POLLY'S PERFECT PET

A Pet Yoga Book for Kids

Written by Giselle Shardlow
Illustrated by Lauren Hughes

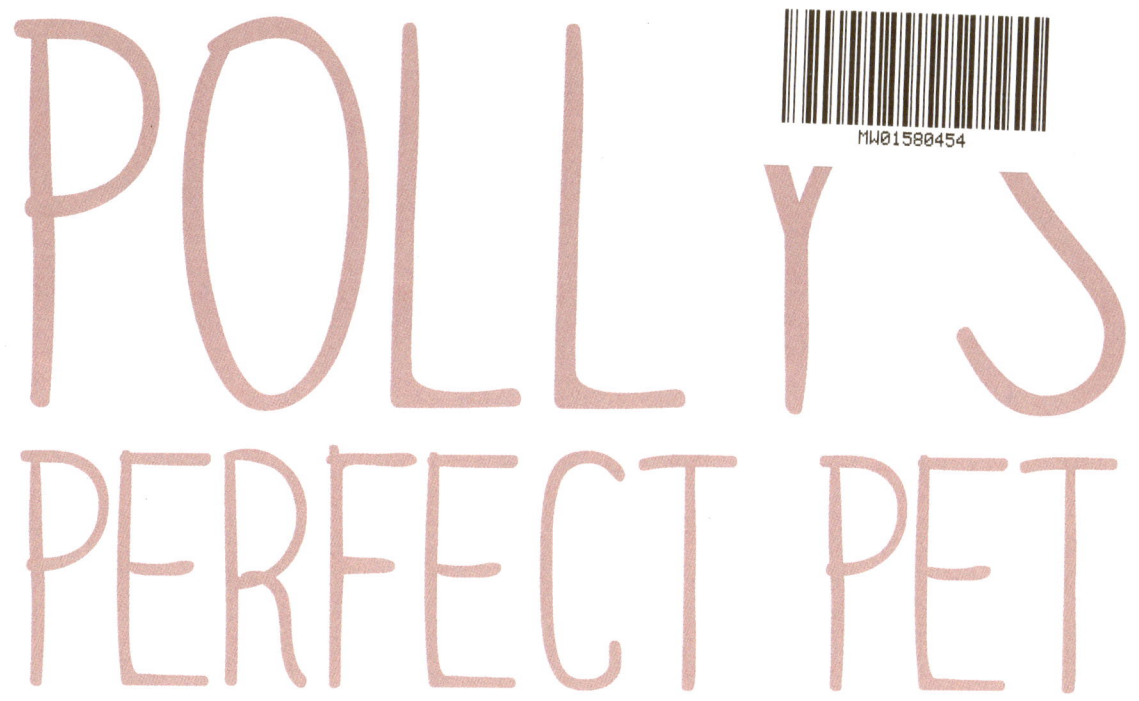

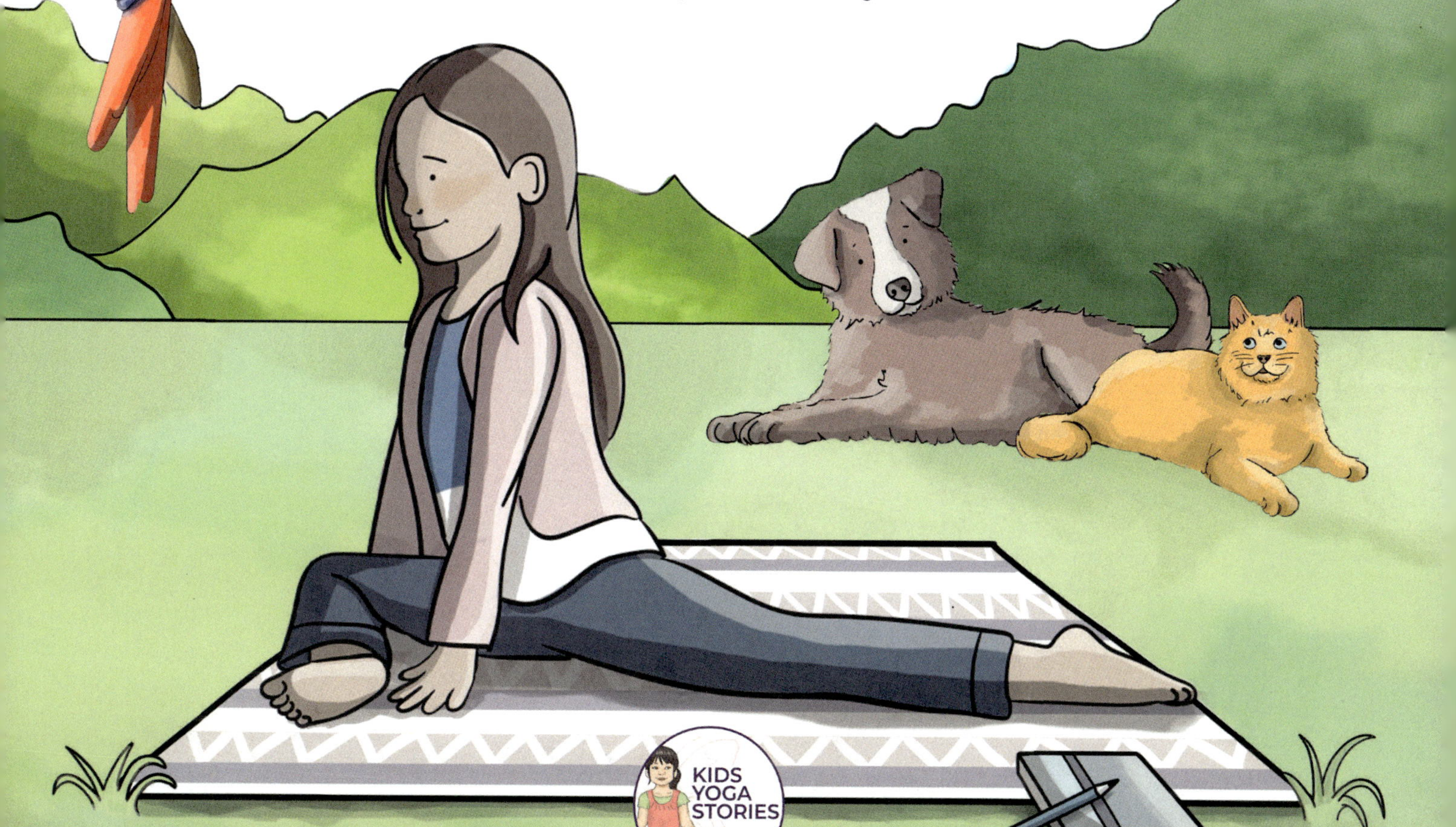

KIDS YOGA STORIES
kidsyogastories.com

For all the pet-loving children in our neighborhood. ~G.S.

Copyright © 2021 by Giselle Shardlow
Illustrations by Lauren Hughes
All images © 2021 Giselle Shardlow

All rights reserved. No part of this book may be reproduced in any form by any electronic or mechanical means, including photocopying, recording, or information storage and retrieval without written permission from the author. The author, illustrator, and publisher accept no responsibility or liability for any injuries or losses that may result from practicing the yoga poses outlined in this storybook. Please ensure your own safety and the safety of the children.

ISBN-13: 978-1-943648-62-7 (print)

Kids Yoga Stories
Boston, MA
www.kidsyogastories.com
www.amazon.com/author/giselleshardlow
Email us at info@kidsyogastories.com.

Ordering Information: Special discounts are available on quantity purchases by contacting the publisher at the email address above.

What do you think? Let us know what you think of *Polly's Perfect Pet* at feedback@kidsyogastories.com.

Printed in the United States of America.

How to Use This Yoga Book for Kids

Welcome to Kids Yoga Stories. Our yoga books are designed to integrate learning, movement, and fun. Below are a few tips for getting the most out of this pet yoga book:

1. **Flip** through the story to familiarize yourself with the format. Pay special attention to the characters' movements on each page and the corresponding yoga keywords. The list of keywords and yoga pose instructions can be found at the end of the book.

2. **Read** the story with your child, but this time, act out the story as you go along. Use the illustrations of Polly practicing the poses as a guide. Encourage your child's imagination.

3. **Refer** to the list of yoga poses for kids and the parent-teacher guide at the back of the book for further information.

Enjoy your yoga story, but please be safe!

Polly looked up from the book she was **reading**. It was about cats.

"I'd love to get another pet, Mom!"

"Would you now?" Her mom looked over from the kitchen.
"Well, you have been very responsible with your fish.
And I just saw a flyer for a pet fair in the park today.
Let's go and research some pets to see which one might be a good fit."

"Great idea! Thanks, Mom!"

Polly jumped up to grab her notebook and pencil.

Polly and her mom headed into town.

Riding in the car, Polly was bursting with excitement.

At the park, people were setting up for the pet fair.

"I hope we find the right pet for us, Mom!" said Polly.

"Me too," said Mom, with a smile.

At the first table, Polly's friend Connor had a little box with a heat lamp.

"Hi, Polly! Would you like to meet our new chick? We love our **chickens** and collect eggs every day!"

"She's so cute." Polly made a note in her book about chickens laying eggs, but then she remembered Connor saying in class that he worried about the coyotes getting the chickens.

Having fresh eggs would be terrific, but she would have to figure out how to keep the chickens safe.

Crescent Lunge Pose

Polly and her mom continued on to the second table, where a girl was cuddling a **puppy**.

"Aw, Mom, he's sooo cute!" Polly gushed, kneeling to pet the little dog.

"Isn't he adorable?" The girl yawned, brushing fur off her shirt. "But I'm exhausted. He's been keeping us up all night with his barking."

Polly made notes under her column labelled "puppy."

She couldn't imagine being kept up all night! Maybe a new puppy wasn't worth the lost sleep.

At the next table, Polly saw her best friend Mikah with a fluffy cat.

"Hi, Mrs. Williams," Mikah said. "Polly has been telling me that she wants a pet that's not a fish."

"I've heard the same thing." Mom laughed.

"This is Lily," Polly said. "She's so fun to play with! We chase her around the house, and she loves to play with her little cat toys."

Mikah whispered, "Yes, she's super fun, but my mom is mad at her for scratching our new couch. Whoops!"

"Oh no! Unfortunately, we can't have a **cat** because of my husband's allergies," Mom explained.

Polly made another note in her book. *Dad's allergies make this decision even harder,* she thought.

"Oh, look, Polly! There's a jazz band. Let's listen for a bit," Mom said.

They laid out their **picnic blanket** and unpacked their snacks.

Polly also updated her notebook and thought about the first three pets she'd seen so far: chickens, a puppy, and a cat.

She had notes in both the "positive" and "negative" columns for each pet. Choosing the perfect pet involved a lot of research.

"Ready to keep looking?" Mom asked as they packed up the blanket.

"Yes! Let's go see Pete." Polly ran to the table where their neighbor, Mrs. Byrd, waited with her **parrot**, Pete.

"Polly want a cracker! *Gaawk*!" Pete screeched.

Pigeon Pose

"Oh, Polly, so lovely to see you here!" Mrs. Byrd said, flashing her famous smile.

Polly sometimes helped Mrs. Byrd with errands and had gotten to know Pete.

She loved him, but also knew what an awful mess he made in Mrs. Byrd's kitchen. Plus, his screeches were super loud. Polly didn't love loud noises.

"Great to see you too, Mrs. Byrd," Polly answered. "We're here researching pets."

"You'll make the right choice. I have no doubt!" Mrs. Byrd said.

As they approached the next table,
Polly recognized an older boy from her school.

"Would you like to hold my guinea pig?" James asked.

"Sure," Polly said as she picked up the little animal and gently stroked its head. "Oh! He's so soft!"

"I wanted a cat, but my mom is allergic, so we got two guinea pigs instead," James explained. "I really like them, actually."

Polly remembered reading that **guinea pigs** liked to live in pairs, so that would be twice the food and twice the work.

"Just remember: guinea pigs are cute and cuddly, but they make a big mess, and they sometimes smell." James shrugged. "It's a trade-off, right?"

Child's Pose

"Yes, we're learning all about trade-offs."
Polly winked at her mom then wrote some notes in her book.

Mom winked back. "We'll keep looking, though."

Back at home, Polly **reviewed her notes** from the pet fair.

"Well, we can't have a cat or dog because of dad's allergies. We can't get a turtle, guinea pig, or bunny because they make messes and are smelly."

Polly was starting to realize that owning a pet would be hard work. But she felt determined to keep going.

She really wanted a pet to love and care for.

"We can't get a parrot, because it's too loud. And you can't cuddle a fish."

Polly rubbed her head, then she beamed. "But there is one option left!"

"I've actually been thinking about getting chickens!"

Mom smiled and placed a hand on Polly's shoulder. "I talked to Connor's mom about how to get them set up and how to clean the coop. If we split up the duties, then I think our family could manage it. And once the **chicks** grow up, we'd get fresh eggs every day!"

"Chickens! That would be so fun!" Polly cheered.

"Let's see…
 The baby chicks are so cute,
 we have room in the backyard,
 and I can collect the **eggs** every day."

"Let's go find Dad!"

That night in bed, Polly thought about her exciting day.

She had learned so much about the different pets.

She drifted off to sleep, thinking about the adorable baby chicks that would soon be part of her family.

Resting Pose

A Day at the Pet Fair

A Day at the Pet Fair

List of Yoga Poses for Kids

#	Keyword	Yoga Pose	Demonstration
1	Reading	Easy Pose	
2	Riding in a car	Chair Pose	
3	Chickens	Crescent Lunge Pose	
4	Puppy	Downward-Facing Dog Pose	
5	Cat	Cat Pose	
6	Kneeling on a picnic blanket	Hero Pose	

List of Yoga Poses for Kids

#	Keyword	Yoga Pose	Demonstration
7	Parrot	Pigeon Pose	
8	Guinea Pigs	Child's Pose	
9	Looking in a notebook	Cobbler's Pose	
10	Chicks	Squat Pose	
11	Eggs	Knees-to-Chest Pose	
12	Lying in bed	Resting Pose	

How to Practice the Yoga Poses

The following list is intended as a guide only. Please encourage the children's creativity while ensuring their safety.

1. Easy Pose: Sit cross-legged and rest your palms on your knees. Close your eyes, if you are comfortable doing so. Take a few deep breaths and relax your body. Pretend to be reading a book.

2. Chair Pose: Stand tall in Mountain Pose with your feet hip-width apart, bend your knees, and keep a straight spine. Hold your hands out in front of you. Pretend to be riding in a car.

3. Crescent Lunge: From a standing position, step your right foot back into a lunge with your left foot directly over your left knee and a straight back leg. Inhale and take your parallel arms straight up overhead. Open your chest, look up, and take a few deep breaths. Pretend to be a chicken. Switch sides and repeat the steps.

4. Downward-Facing Dog Pose: From all fours, lift your knees to an upside-down V shape, with your buttocks up in the air. Ensure that your palms are flat on the ground and that your spine and legs are straight. Press your heels toward the ground and look back through your legs. Pretend to be a puppy.

5. Cat Pose: On all fours, round your back and tuck your chin into your chest. Pretend to be a cat.

6. Hero Pose: Come to rest upright on your heels with your palms resting on your knees. Pretend to be kneeling on a picnic blanket.

7. Pigeon Pose: From an all-fours position, bring your right knee to rest behind your right hand, angling your right foot slightly inward. Gently take your buttocks down to the ground with your left leg extended straight out behind you. You might try placing a block under your right thigh. Keep your palms flat on the ground on either side of your right knee, look forward, keeping a straight spine. Pretend to be a parrot. Repeat on the other side.

8. Child's Pose: Sit on your heels, slowly bring your forehead down to rest on the floor in front of your knees, rest your arms down alongside your body, and take a few deep breaths. Pretend to be a guinea pig.

9. Cobbler's Pose: Sit on your buttocks with a tall spine, bend your legs, place the soles of your feet together. Pretend to be looking in a notebook.

10. Squat Pose: Come down to a squat with your knees apart and your arms between your knees. Touch your hands to the ground. Pretend to be a chick.

11. Knees-to-Chest Pose: Lie on your back, bend your knees, and hug them close to your chest. Pretend to be an egg.

12. Resting Pose: Lie on your back with your arms and legs stretched out. Pretend to be lying in bed. Breathe and rest.

Parent-Teacher Guide

This guide contains tips to get the most out of your experience of yoga stories with young children.

Put safety first. Ensure that the space is clear and clean. Spend some time clearing any dangerous objects or unnecessary items. Wear comfortable clothing and practice barefoot.

Props are welcome. Yoga mats or towels (on a non-slip surface) are optional. Pet-related props and pet-themed music are good additions.

Cater to the age group. Use this Kids Yoga Stories book as a guide, but make adaptations according to the age of your children. Feel free to lengthen or shorten your journey to ensure that your children are fully engaged throughout your time together. We recommend reading this book with children ages four to seven (preschoolers to early primary).

Talk together. Engage your children in the book's topic. Talk about what they know about various pets and if they actually own one so they can form meaningful connections. Explain the purpose of yoga stories—to integrate movement, reading, and fun.

Learn through movement. Brain research shows that we learn best through physical activity. Our bodies are designed to be active. Encouraging your children to act out the keywords allows them to have fun while learning about different pets. Use repetition to engage the children and help them learn the movements. Ask your child to say or predict the next pose in their pretend visit to a pet fair.

Develop breath awareness. Throughout the practice, bring the children's attention to the action of inhaling and exhaling in a light-hearted way. For example, encourage the children to join Polly in taking a deep breath while kneeling on the picnic blanket. Have the children close their eyes (if that's comfortable) while in Hero Pose. Take a moment to pause the story and reflect on what Polly has learned so far. Then take a few deep breaths at the end of the book as the readers pretend to be lying in bed.

Relax. Allow your children time to end their session in Resting Pose for five to ten minutes. You could even follow the story with a pet-themed relaxation story. Massage their feet during or after their relaxation period. Relaxation techniques give children a way to deal with stress. Reinforce the benefits and importance of quiet time for their minds and bodies. Introduce meditation, which can be as simple as sitting quietly for a couple of minutes, as a way to bring stillness to their highly stimulated lives.

Lighten up and enjoy yourself. A children's yoga experience is not as formal as an adult class. Encourage the children to use their creativity and provide them time to explore the postures. Avoid teaching perfectly aligned poses. The journey is intended to be joyful and fun. Your children feed off your passion and enthusiasm. So take the opportunity to energize yourself, as well. Read and act out the yoga book together as a way to connect with each other.

About Kids Yoga Stories

We hope you enjoyed your Kids Yoga Stories experience. Visit **www.kidsyogastories.com** to:

Receive updates. For yoga tips, printables, and kids yoga resources, sign up for our free Kids Yoga Stories Newsletter.

Connect with us. Please share with us about your yoga journey. Send pictures of yourself practicing the poses or reading the story. Describe your journey on our social media pages (Facebook, Pinterest, Instagram, and Twitter).

Check out free stuff. Read our articles on books, yoga, parenting, and travel. Download one of our kids yoga lesson plans or coloring pages.

Read or write a review. Read what others have to say about our yoga books for kids or post your own review on Amazon or on our website. We would love to hear how you enjoyed this yoga book.

Thank you for your support in spreading our message of integrating learning, movement, and fun.

Giselle

Kids Yoga Stories
www.kidsyogastories.com
giselle@kidsyogastories.com
www.pinterest.com/kidsyogastories
www.facebook.com/kidsyogastories

www.twitter.com/kidsyogastories
www.amazon.com/author/giselleshardlow
www.goodreads.com/giselleshardlow
www.instagram.com/kidsyogastories

About the Author

Giselle Shardlow draws from her experiences as a teacher, traveler, mother, and yogi to write her yoga stories for children. The purpose of her yoga books is to foster happy, healthy, and globally educated children. She lives in Boston with her husband and daughter.

About the Illustrator

Lauren Hughes resides in Gloucestershire, England. Her love for the outdoors and exploring nature can be seen throughout her work, with animals and flowers making frequent appearances. Her aim is to inspire and educate people through her drawings, to evoke emotions, and to enhance understanding on many different levels.

OTHER YOGA BOOKS FOR KIDS
By Giselle Shardlow

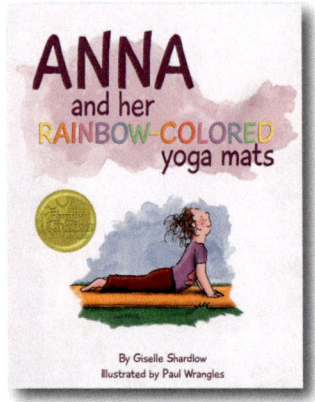
Anna and Her Rainbow-Colored Yoga Mats

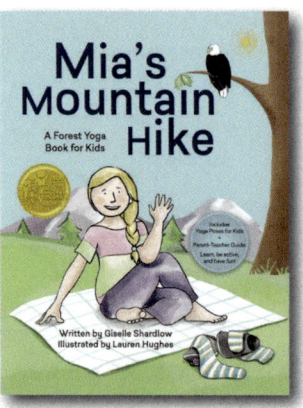
Mia's Mountain Hike

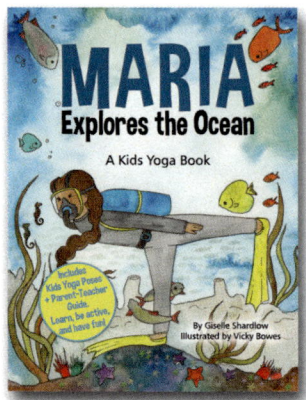
Maria Explores the Ocean

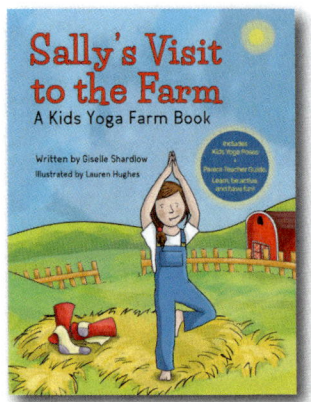
Sally's Visit to the Farm

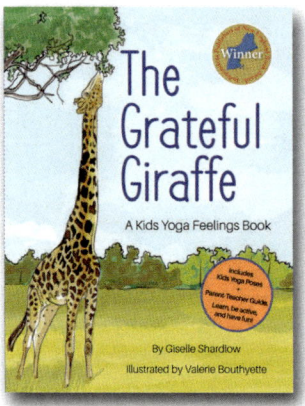
The Grateful Giraffe

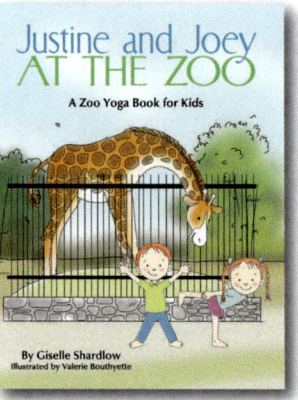
Justine and Joey at the Zoo

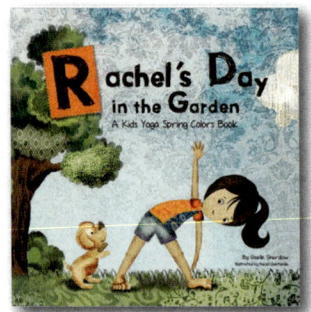
Rachel's Day in the Garden

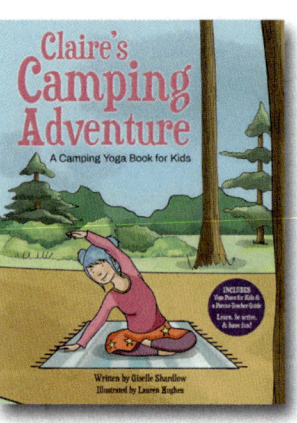
Claire's Camping Adventure

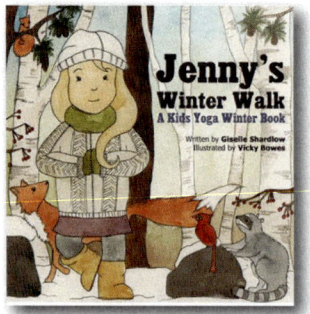
Jenny's Winter Walk

The yoga books above are available in paperback or digital download formats.

BUY YOUR YOGA BOOKS HERE:
shop.kidsyogastories.com

Made in the USA
Coppell, TX
14 April 2023

15617369R00029